Make Money From Home:

15 Quick and Easy techniques on how you can make massive amount of money online

By Calvin Kennedy

©Copyright 2016 WE CANT BE BEAT LLC

Copyright 2016 by Calvin Kennedy.

Published by WE CANT BE BEAT LLC

Krob817@yahoo.com

Table of Contents

Make Money From Home: 1

Chapter 1: Introduction 4

Chapter 2: Finding Your Niche 16

Chapter 3: 3 Low Impact Methods to Generate Income Online 23

Chapter 4: The Basics 32

Chapter 5: The Facts 38

Chapter 6: The Options 43

Conclusion 102

Technical Terms and Definition 107

Chapter 1: Introduction

Do you hear people saying that they are making a great living online, and wish you could too? Right now we are in the midst of a time of change. Traditional manufacturing jobs are on the decline, and even jobs in service industries are harder to find.

However, there are thousands of new ways to earn money on the internet. Plus many of these new ideas for earning can be started part-time, from the comfort of your home, alongside raising a family. More and more, successful people are adapting to the new economic climate, not just by ditching the idea of a job for life, but also by ceasing to rely on a single job for all their income. This does require a change in the way you think. You need to be open to opportunities and be ready to learn. Online earning is only successful for those who persist. If earning online sounds like something that you would love to do, and you are ready to commit some time and effort to the process, read on. There is hard work ahead of you, but the benefits are immense. You can work from anywhere in the world, at the times of day that suit you. Making money online is ideal if you are restricted to working limited hours, whether it is because you have another job, a health condition that stops you going out to work or you are at home looking after the family. Beyond that, it can allow you to take time out, travel, have the school holidays off and more, as long as you set up how you earn correctly.

ANYONE CAN DO IT ... WITH SOME EXPERT ADVICE

Whether you view online marketing experts with suspicion or awe, there are lots of people making big claims right now. To get the most out of this book, we want to share our experiences with you, as well as those of other internet experts. So, to get started, read how we both learned, through trial and error, how to earn our livings online.

THE 'MAKING MONEY' MINDSET

Throughout this book, we won't just be teaching you practical techniques for online earning, though there are plenty of those courses and books out there. We will be asking you to change the way you think, indeed to forget everything you have been taught about work and earning money. The way you think is called a **'mindset'** and later on you can read about developing a helpful mindset to make learning easier. If you want to start earning online, you will soon find other people making dismissive comments. Ignore the people who say it is impossible to 'have it all.' The sad truth is that some people do not want to see you succeed because it calls into question the decisions they have made and continue to make, let them make the decisions for themselves and you can concentrate on making great decisions for yourself. Coach Allison Marlowe says: I have been on my personal development journey for around 15 years. Now and then I take a quantum leap. I do not worry anymore about the money: my experience is when I step up, I just go with it. I have an unwritten rule that when I do invest big, I make that money back within a couple of months. I paid £15,000 to join a group and made £18,000 back within a couple of months. The knowledge that I have is valuable to other people. I know it inside out, upside down. People are buying me, buying my time, buying my expertise. Once you can get your head around the fact that what you know is not known to everybody, it is a gift, and other people do value it. I believe that I deserve to ask for money in return for that. When I think small, it does not work. When I put my prices up, more people recommend me.

YOUR GOALS

Before you start earning online, get clear in your mind why you are doing this and what you want to achieve. This will make it easier for you to stay on track and concentrate on activities that get you closer to your goal. Ask yourself, 'What do I want?' You could be looking for a bit of spare cash that just means you have enough money for treats or to avoid going overdrawn. You might be looking for a part-time income instead of getting a job, or so you can cut down your hours. Alternatively, you might be studying or caring for family and in need of a flexible income that allows you to work around your regular commitments. Maybe, like us, you have the goal of earning a full-time income on part-time hours. We are living proof that this can be done, and we want to share that with you. All the things you will learn in this book are concepts and strategies that we use day in, day out to make four figures a month in just ten or twenty hours' work a week. We are not writing about any 'get rich quick' scheme. If you need a sum of money right now, then please make a boot sale or look for a job. What you will learn from this book is a long-term strategy, not a 'make £1,000 in 24 hours' scam. If you have had enough of being beholden to bosses, juggling childcare, having no spare cash, feeling that you are not contributing financially or struggling with debt, then read on, because what we have to say could change your life.

LIFE CHANGE STARTS HERE

We have three essential concepts that we want you to understand before moving on to the rest of this book. Get these ideas right and you will have taken the first step to changing the way you earn money so it can be done right now make the commitments.

Concept 1: multiple streams of income. The first idea that will change the way you think about earning is multiple streams of revenue there are lots to this topic, which will become evident as you read through the book but let's start with a short explanation.

Think about what is happening in the world right now. Business owners are going out of business and employees are being fired left and right. For those people, that business or job was their sole source of income. Does the idea that your entire life is dependent on one source of revenue make you feel uncomfortable? It should. You can end up in dire straits through no fault of your own, such as when the recession took hold. Gone are the days when jobs were for life and large establishments like Woolworths thought they could never go down. We do not want to be a scaremonger, far from it, but times have changed, and it is the time we changed with them. Imagine this alternative scenario: Sharon worked on the till at Woolies twenty hours a week, but she also has some online incomes. She writes a parenting blog that earns her £300 a month in advertising. She does some freelance writing for £150 per month. Sharon's also just launched an eBook from a blog in a niche area which earns £75 a month and she's in the process of launching an eCourse. Woolies go bust in the recession and what does Sharon do? Sharon cuts back and lives off her other incomes. She spends her free time creating that eCourse which grows to earn her around £300 a month and she invested her redundancy money in another business opportunity which she hopes will be a big success. No matter which of Sharon's incomes disappears she has others on which to rely, and it is highly unlikely that all her incomes will dry up at the same time. This is the theory behind multiple streams of revenue. What does this mean for you? It means you do not need one big idea or lots of investment to cease being reliant on an employer. If you are a business owner, it takes a lot of the risk out of being an entrepreneur as, instead of relying on one idea or one market, you have some enterprises. This might sound like a big commitment, but in this book we explain how you can build up an online income incrementally while still working or alongside your other commitments. This is exactly what we have done: we have made our profits up gradually to a point where our 'work' is flexible, and our benefits are multiple.

What do you think of this concept?

Concept 2: Passive income. So, has the idea of multiple income streams got you thinking? You might be thinking, 'Great, when can I start?' or you might be wondering just how you find time to generate several different ways of earning when right now you are struggling with just one. Concept two, passive income, is going to stop you worrying right now. What is passive income? Different people have a slightly different definition as to what constitutes passive income. For us, it is income that comes from a source that does not require ongoing work. So interest from your ISA would be classed as passive income, as would the appreciation of your valuables. Our passive incomes include affiliate marketing income, eBooks, eCourses, sidebar advertising and membership subscriptions. All of these incomes do not require a time commitment every day. These incomes continue to flow regardless of your input. It is worth investing time upfront in creating this sort of ongoing income. As examples, we had written books and created eCourses and directories, in the knowledge that our time invested upfront will create a permanent passive income. Passive income is one reason why the 'rich always get richer' or why 'money goes to money.' With the internet, you too have the opportunity to create these passive incomes for yourself. What passive incomes do you currently have? How can you maximize your passive income? Think of ways online and offline: you will get lots of ideas as you work through this book.

Concept 3: leveraging your time.
Concept three will help you make the most of whatever time you have, whether it is a few hours at evenings and weekends, or ninety minutes each day while your toddler naps. Leverage your time by starting to move away from selling your time by the hour. You can only go so far when you are selling your time as you only have so long to sell! Leverage your time by finding someone you can pay to do activities for less than the income they generate. If you are setting up an online shop and have hundreds of products to load onto the shop, it will be more cost effective to find someone else to do this

while you get on with promoting the store. If you have a business and are doing your accounts you could work more effectively by finding a bookkeeper and getting on with using your skills where they are most effective. There are much more ways to leverage your time. If you are a coach, for example, you might offer group coaching where you can coach some people at once rather than simply working one to one. If you own business, franchising will move you on from 'doing it all' to having some other people who are all contributing to your income.

Leverage your products and knowledge

If you have extensive knowledge on a topic, you can take advantage of your time by creating an eBook. You write the book once, but it can be sold many times over without further commitment from you. Your expertise could also be used to create an eCourse that can be delivered automatically. Keep thinking of ways to leverage what you already have in a way that can earn you a passive income.

Leverage your income - Invest some of the income you make into training and other business ideas. Always stay one step ahead. Get into the habit of investing a percentage of your income into training and new ventures. We always find training to be money well spent. We can learn what we need to maximize our earnings in the future. Sometimes the first investment is the hardest because that's coming direct from your pocket.

WHAT NEXT? So, now you know how we have created our flexible incomes. Plus, you have started to learn about three essential concepts that will allow you to earn online in a flexible way. Now it is time to get stuck into learning about the practical techniques you will need to make your first few pounds online.

Chapter 2: Finding Your Niche

WHY HAVE A NICHE?

You might be raring to go, all ready to find ways to make money online, but first I am going to ask you a question. Why should people buy from you? Unless you have something to offer that is unique and different, any attempts to make money online are going to be mostly wasted as you struggle to get yourself noticed in crowded marketplaces. If you can find a niche with little competition and become known as the person to go to for relevant information, products and services; you will be in a strong position to make money.

Helen Lindop has spent some years researching niches for entrepreneurs. She explains why a niche is a good idea: You do not have the time or the money to reach out to a wide range of buyers, so you need your promotional activities to be focused in one place. 'Niching' can be scary, though. It is tempting to try to be all things to all people because you do not want to lose customers. The trouble with this is that if you do not know exactly who your customers are, you can't go to the places they hang out. And you can't explain to them that you have got a fab new widget that will solve a pressing problem of theirs. Having a niche does not mean you have to turn other people away. Your niche is the focus of your promotional efforts rather than a strict rule about who you can sell to. Here's another big advantage: if you have got a niche, you can become an expert in your chosen area much faster than you would otherwise. Given the choice, wouldn't you go to the specialist first?

HOW TO FIND A NICHE

Now, let's get down to the nuts and bolts of finding a niche. Your first thought when looking into making money online may be to find a nice big niche with lots of searches, something like 'online dating' or 'weight loss,' but it can be hard to make an impact in this sort of crowded market, however, many people there are searching. If you think of your behavior when searching online, do you often look beyond the first page of search engine results? You need to find a focused niche where you can achieve a listing on the first page of search engine results for a site to make you money, ideally where you are the first three results. To do this, you need to do keyword research. Once you have a broad idea of an area that you might focus on, start looking at the keywords potential customers might search on. Enter these into something like the Google Keyword Tool. Google 'free keyword tool for AdWords' or paste this into your browser: https://adwords.google.com/select/KeywordToolExternal. It will come up with a range of suggestions for similar keywords, phrases that include your keywords and more. Pick a phrase, drill down by adding in further words to make your phrase more accurate, and explore similar phrases with slightly different wording. Assess the number of searches and the degree of competition as indicated by the Keyword Tool. You are looking for phrases with a moderate search volume, at least several thousand per month and with as little competition as possible. If your phrase relates to something you can supply globally look at the global searches, if not, look at the local searches. This is not quite as simple as it seems: search volumes can differ depending on whether you are logged in or logged out of the Google tool. The Keyword Tool does not show search volumes. It shows 'the approximate 12-month average of user queries for the keyword on Google.co.uk and the Google Search Network', which can lead to inflated search volumes, and data based on searches a few months ago. So, alongside using the Keyword Tool, search on Google and see what 'autocomplete' terms appear. For example, if you are searching for 'Keep calm and ...' you will find that when you type just those three words into a Google search box, it suggests firstly 'Keep Calm and Carry On', but, at the time of writing, this is swiftly fol-lowed by 'Keep Calm and Be Reem', a catchphrase from The Only Way is Essex TV show. This phrase wouldn't have appeared in the top search terms even a few months earlier. Google Autocomplete gives different results on the Google web search page, which is based on search volumes over some months to the Google news search page, which is based on current search terms. By checking your possible phrases in all these places, you can assess whether you have a phrase worth optimizing for. Once you have some ideas for the main phrases surrounding your potential niche, type them into a range of different search engines. How many web pages appear when you search? Examine the top ranking sites on the first page of results. Check out some of the lower ranking pages and see what they might be missing.

Tools to help with niche research
There are various online tools to assist you with researching keywords and niches. Starting very simply, look at Rob Millard's Keyword Expander, http://www.rob-millard.com/keyword-expander, which helps you drill down from keywords and phrases and check trends for use

in Google searches over the years. You can also download further tools including Micro Niche Finder, HTTP:// www.micronichefinder.com, and Market Samurai, http://www.marketsamurai.com, which claim to help you find untapped niches.

A person-centered approach
Helen Lindop advises, the trick is to find a group of people that
a) Already hang out together and
b) Want something that you have. Why? Well, it is a lot easier to find your customers and talk to them as a group if they are already meeting up, reading the same websites or buying the same magazines. Plus it is easier to sell to them if you have a solution to one of their problems than if you think you have got something they might like.

MONEY MAKING NICHES.
Once you have some ideas for a niche focused on certain key phrases, assess whether it is one that

will have the potential to make you money. An easy-to- monetize niche is one that is
- product-focused
- full of buyers with a reasonable amount of disposable income
- under-serviced
- already making money for other people

Chapter 3: 3 Low Impact Methods to Generate Income Online

With today's unstable economy, people are finding that it's best to have multiple streams of income. Working online can generate part-time or full-time payouts. This job can also be tailored to an already busy work schedule and can be done within the spare time you have throughout the day.

There is a lot of work available for those wanting to work online, but many of the popular jobs are taken, in customer service or a scam. So, some of the opportunities or jobs that will be discussed here don't have a money cap, meaning you can make as much as you want to depend on the level of time and effort you put into it.

Teespring

Teespring is perfect for the creative people out there and for those with no startup money to invest in an online opportunity. Designing t-shirts and finding an audience to sell them to are all you have to do. Then the company will make them, distribute them to customers, and then you get paid.

There are over 10,000 clip art options to choose from or for the creative; you can upload your images. If there ever was a great saying that hasn't been put onto a shirt or a design that you think would be highly demanded, Teespring is the place to test it out.

Getting started with Teespring is easy. All you have to do is start a campaign. With this campaign, design a shirt, determine how many shirts need to be ordered before production begins, and think about the pricing of the shirts and for how long you wish to run the campaign. After all that is taken care of, the next thing to do would be to spread the word about your awesome new shirts. Telling friends, family, making flyers, business cards or using social media are all ways to spread the word about the campaign.

This method is known as crowd funding and has become very popular. The goal is to make something that the people want, and they help fund the dream. This method has helped a lot of new products get launched. This can be a very lucrative way to make money, especially if you create something new, meaningful and attractive. Working with a reputable company like Teespring ensures excellent quality and customer service, so your clients will have a good experience as well when shopping with this company.

Google Helpouts

Having a skill that can be helpful to others is another great way to capitalize online. People are willing to pay for your services. One of the most recent popular options is Google Helpouts. Here you can charge per minute or increments of fifteen minutes and offer a skill. Anything you can think of can be potentially provided in Google Helpouts. Everything from exercising, weight loss, math, WordPress, cooking, fashion tips, business advice and much more. It's a pool of skilled individuals that offer their skills at competitive prices. After you have a good amount of ratings, people will flock to you for help.

Getting started with Google Helpouts is relatively straightforward. You do need to know how to conduct live video calls because that is how each session takes place. It doesn't cost any upfront fees to get started. You have the option of giving help for free or charging for help. Now since the goal is to make money online, you'll most likely want to charge for help. Browse other providers that do something similar to yourself and see what they charge and get an idea of what you need to charge.

This route can be competitive and get the first client might be difficult if you are priced too high.

Google Helpouts are a little different than other online opportunities because this doesn't require any extra work. You could go out your way to promote yourself, but it's already a part of a huge audience, and the people will come to you. After a few reviews, you won't have to do much but own your skills and wait for people to need your services. The more good reviews, the more people will come to you for help. Just make sure your scenery is always professional and that there aren't any distractions when you are taking video calls.

Udemy

One of the best things to do to make more money is learning a new skill. It's less expensive than going to college and at the same time, you'll learn from instructors that do exactly what they are teaching. It's the best hands on experience you can find. The instructors are some of the best in the field and can help you add on to your skills or help you learn a new one. These courses are business driven and are there to help reach more professional goals. They are meant to teach skills that can be used for fun but most importantly to make a profit as well. Getting started is simple as you just need to search what you want to do and pay for the course. Learn a new skill and use it to help you reach your financial goals by teaching what you learned to others in need.

Becoming an instructor is also possible if you live close by. They are always hiring and if it's a good fit for you apply, and that too can be another stream of income.

Benefits of working at home

Working from home is an all glorious and an incredible undertaking. The thought of working from home and earning some income is now a reality. Most of the lucrative businesses are today being carried out from home and as a result, many private premises have been turned into offices.

The choice to start working from home is done after a careful investigation and consideration. If you will finally make that purposeful selection of starting to make some income from the comfort of your home, then, you will realize that it has some of these benefits;

-Time - A person who works from home can spend much of the time with the family members. For example, a working mom will be able to interact more closely with her kids, and monitor their progress. However, you need to have time management skills because spending more time with members of your family could mean more interruptions which in turn reduces output on your online job.

-Self-employment- A person who works from home is no doubt his boss. One has high flexibility as he can choose what, when and how to do the assignments.

-Improved productivity- One is also likely to do more work by converting his private room at home into an office. Reduced movements and fewer interruptions as in the case of a conventional office are minimized. Further, you can work at any time of the day, meaning that odd hours and days can be converted into productive working days.

-Improved quality of life- There are many jobs available online. Some of these jobs, e.g. freelancing have helped to supplement income by earning extra money from writing articles. Others have left their regular day jobs altogether to work on online platforms.

-Reduced stress- Some jobs are not only stressing, but also annoying. The pressures may come from the employer or even the colleagues. Working from home reduces the frequency of interaction with these groups and makes your job more enjoyable.

-A healthier lifestyle- You will be able to enjoy a quality lifestyle right from the comfort of your home. Through a schedule, you will be able to exercise and eat the proper diet, all of which forms a recipe for a healthy lifestyle.

-Saving on the startup costs- The capital outlays required to start businesses are in most cases, prohibitive. However, most of these initial costs are eliminated mainly for the fledgling online marketers.

Chapter 4: The Basics

Plan

Get some business plan; the straightforward plan then writes down what you would like to do to earn your money is it with selling, your personal website, blogging, etc. Build your ideas on paper so you can visualize it, know how you want to do it, write down your ideas, goals, how much you are prepared to spend, how many hours you can spend each day, etc. Choose something and give it your all, put your energy on that one idea. Don't start off with different ideas. For instance pick a topic you know best and that you love if you want to start a website or blog, and focus on that particular topic. So to plan it, know what you want to sell, what topic you have sound knowledge of, what interest you most.

Be motivated

You cannot do something if you are not going to enjoy it – that's what's going to keep you motivated. If you are not motivated by what you are doing your scheme might fail, that's not what you want. Nobody can give you an estimated time in which you will start earning money, so stay motivated, keep improving and you'll bear the fruit of your success. Times can be hard, and it's not always easy to stay motivated if you are already in need of some income. Maybe that's why you started looking for ways to make money online and quick. Get into it seriously and you will make a success! If you feel it's not working, you are never going to get an income, don't stop, keep going; you will find that the longer you do it, the easier it will get.

Be patient

Stay positive it might not be easy in the beginning; you are new at this, and you still have a lot to learn. Never give up, even if it takes you months to get set-up and to go. It all takes time, but once you start making money with your online business it can grow (maybe not as quick as you hoped for but with time you'll become more successful) remember you are one small individual that has to make a mark in a huge global society. Don't worry about that; just be patient, because it will take the time to get your website up there where it will attract millions of visitors. Please don't say it will be impossible to get noticed on the internet no with traffic you will be just as good as any other website already existing on the web. Just give it time!

Do research

If you need more information about a particular idea, ask people with experience, do research on search engines. Ask around, on some sites; you can read their FAQ (frequently asked questions), read other web users experiences on the particular kind of business or market. You can never have enough information. So keep searching even when you started your online business, keep looking for better-improved ways of doing it, new traffic attracting ways, etc. Research stays part of your business; you want to stay on top of new methods, so even when you have your business running already keep doing research.

Careful of scams

I have never come across any 'get rich quick' scheme that works as good as they promise. Don't fall for the schemes that make it sound so easy; you'll have to put in a lot of effort to make money. You earn a commission, but only when you upgrade to a higher level (with membership fees involved), you will earn a better commission and then still it is going to be a lot of work. If you read about all the right successful online money making schemes, you'll find that it's not as glamorous as they advertised. Most are a catch to get more people registering. You will have to work very hard to earn any money. I don't say don't try it out; you can try it out, see how it works, but stay realistic. You can learn from the experience.

Don't be afraid

Go for it! Don't let your fears stop you from making a success. You can make a success maybe not as quick as you would like but keep in mind you are building your future, your own 'business' being your boss. Any business doesn't matter how big or small, can be a huge success if you have the guts to make it happen. If you are afraid it is going to be a waste of time and money to start your own business, then you are not motivated, which means you are giving up already mentally. You will never know if it is going to work if you are not taking the risk.

Mental Change

Never think you can't do it, or it will be too much work. There are already so many existing online businesses. Remove that mental block that is preventing you from taking that risk. You will never succeed if you don't believe in yourself.

Chapter 5: The Facts

THE TRUTH REVEALED

Ever seen those ads "register now and start earning today"? I always ask myself what's the catch and then wonder what if this is true, what if this one is working? What if! I'm sure you've asked yourself the same? The answer I found was there is no 'get rich overnight scheme' where you earn thousands of dollars within a week or two. Maybe you find the 'special' scheme that actually work, but don't put your hopes on that. There are literally millions of those affiliated market sites on the web. O.K., on the one hand I would, like to tell you not to waste valuable time on those kind of schemes, but on the contrary, it is knowledge and experience that you can learn from those schemes. See how they operate and build your own idea of making money from it perhaps. If you are in serious in need of money then I suggest you rather start your own web page, with your own ads, attracting traffic, because you are going to struggle to make thousands with the "get rich quick' schemes, unless you are very lucky. It will most definitely take some hard work and creativity and dedication from your side to build yourself a really reliable income. Don't get discourage if you fail time and again. Think, get creative and do something you would love to do, it has to make you excited see it as your 'own business'. To give you some idea why it is necessary, if you were opening for example a new coffee shop and you, don't spend time at your coffee shop to see if everything if functioning as you want it to, serve what you customers would like to eat or drink, make it attractive to attract more customers, then your coffee shop will not be as successful agree? It's the same when starting your 'make money business' on the web, you'll need to spend time on it, making it attractive, sell or create something that will be popular and your 'business' will grow over time. So the truth is you will have to put in enough effort to make it work, remember it's going to be your own 'business' so why neglect it?

There is unfortunately no 'push one button, sit back and see the money rolling in scheme', it's not working like that, although some of the 'get rich schemes' promise you some kind of that, it is not that easy and if they promise you something like that then the red lights should start flickering.... stay away or be cautious. As human we all want an easy way out and that's exactly where they catch you. That's what you want, it looks so good and promising, it's hard to resist. All you going to end up with are lots and lots of emails and nothing to show. Step out of that easy way and start working for your money, you are doing it for yourself so be encourage!

THINGS TO LOOK OUT FOR

As mentioned above, watch out for those flashy 'get rich quick' schemes. Most are a scam and some are free but some come at a price. You are going to spend money and be excited to earn loads of money and then you learn you are not going to earn those big bucks overnight and not very soon either. Watch out for scams, because they know how easy it is to catch the vulnerable; the people who are already desperate to earn more money, like mothers who would love to earn money working-from-home. There will always be those out there to prey on the desperate and vulnerable people, and many will fall into the trap. We are only human and the, 'get rich quick' is something that is very attractive to all. If something looks too good to be true do research, luckily we have the internet by a large search engine. Someone might just fell into the same trap and wrote something about the scam. Look it up! Don't give your banking details just to anyone, be sure it is safe. Use other methods of payment or receiving payment, there are more reliable methods on the web, like PayPal. Unfortunately, we live in a world where corruption is everywhere; there are unfortunately scams out there that can steal your money. Just be cautious when you have to provide banking details.

TOP HINTS

When you register for some money making schemes, like marketing, drop ship or auction or any other business, please read the terms and conditions, I know it's not something we care about, but sometimes it is critical to know what the specific requirements are before you are signing up. Yes, you can start a website where you sell stuff, even if you don't have lots of money to invest in your new 'online businesses. I'll recommend a site build option to set up a professional site if you want to promote or sell something. You want your site to look professional it will create a feeling of trust with people.

Chapter 6: The Options

WEBSITES

1.1 Free Websites

You design and create your website, with the help of "free website" websites, comes with free domain and hosting, or minimal fees for hosting, you can also up- grade for more benefits. Designing your own website is not as difficult as you think, it is easy even for beginners. Today there are very easy options on the web to create your own web- site, in your own time, in the comfort of your own home. Don't worry if you don't have enough technical knowledge to create or design a web page, the website where you will create your free website gives you everything you need and they make it easy to use. Search a site that you like and follow the easy to use steps provided to create your very own website. It is also quite fun to create your own website, something you will feel proud of, because you did it yourself. These websites have tons of designs you can edit, to make it your own. No need to worry how to do the set out for your page, like links, pictures, widgets, because it is provided so you can create really anything you need.

You can look for free website creators depending on what you want to achieve with your site. Build websites also offer you to edit and update your website anytime. Depending on different site builders you can publish/upload your website with free domain and hosting, with an affordable option to upgrade with more benefits. I recommend you try it out even just for the fun, even if you don't want to publish your website at first, you might find that it could be fun and that there could be great potential to start your own website.

1.2 Paid websites

 Professional website designers can be contact; the company will design your website professionally, but on the end can be more expensive. If you seriously want to make money it is probably best choice to set up a professional website that will work the best way, depending on what your needs are for your new website . Also depends on how much money you have available to spend on a website. When you have used a website designer to create your site, you will have to pay monthly/ annual fees to host your site. The designing company will maintain your site, so you don't have to about maintenance.

Ups and Downs on website

Ups: There is no excuse not to have your site – free sites are available, and it looks just as professional as a paid designed website.

Downs: It takes time to get your site popular, but it's worth it. You have to do your maintenance on a free site.

2 ONLINE SHOPS

Do you have things to sell? Always an easy way to make money, a very popular site to check out is eBay. It is auction based, but you as seller can make easy money selling items. There is a broad range of ideas of what you can sell, how you want to sell and where you want to sell. When starting an online shop, you have to keep in mind that you will not be the only person selling the same item, which means before buying bulk make sure you can deliver it at a low competitive price. Also make sure there is a high demand out there for the kind of items you are planning on selling.

Here are a few simple ideas when you want to sell online:

3 Wholesale

Find a wholesaler who can deliver goods, buying bulk means you can get products at an excellent retail price. Search around, see which wholesaler can give you best prices and the products you would like to sell of course. Be careful there are some companies out there calling themselves wholesalers, but in fact aren't real wholesalers. If you can't get the items at a retail price then it is probably not such a good idea. When people buy online they want purchase a bargain, and for the buyers it is going to be easy searching online for a better price. To attract people to your site you need to have quality service (like deliver as you promised), high demanding items, and best possible prices. Top 10 items to sell online today are: Books, Computer Hardware, Computer Software, Games, DVD's, Health and Beauty Products, Consumer Electronics, Music and Jewelry.

Ups and downs of wholesale

Ups: Online shopping is getting more popular, more and more people turn to online shopping, because it is convenient and cheaper.

Downs: Getting started may be difficult, there are a lot of new things to learn about online shopping and you need to get traffic to your site to make a success.

4 Drop shipping

When your dream is to start an online shop, but money is a problem, you can look at drop shipping. Drop shipping allows you to have a virtual online store, you don't need a warehouse, staff, and money to buy stock, which means you, can cut on all those expenses selling a product at a lower cost. Some drop ship dealers can help you to set your website up to do drop shipping.

How does it work?

(a) You set up your site with a catalogue of what you are selling. (b) You get the order with payment from your buyer.

(c) You send the order, with your dealer's payment, to your drop ship dealer.

(d) The drop ship dealer does the rest; they do the packaging and delivery.

How do you make money? You sell your product at your own setup price, but you get your product at a retail price which means you pocket the difference between the retail and wholesale price, simple as that.

So what are the risks? You want to keep a good reputation, but you put your reputation in another company's hands. Therefore you have to be sure the drop ship company you choose to deal with, have a good reputation.You have to do a little research before you pick a drop ship dealer. Careful of companies calling themselves drop shippers, some 'drop ship dealers'

Don't deliver or don't give you the products on best retail prices, which means you can't sell your product at a low enough price. Remember you'll have competition out there. You'll have to sell at low prices, and have a good reputation where delivery is concerned.You will stay responsible for the delivery, as your customers will complain with you. Backorders can occur, when products are out of stock and then you'll have to deal with unhappy customers. Know your competitors prices for like products, so you can keep your cost as low as possible.

Ups and downs of drop shipping Ups: If an online shop is your passion, this is a very easy way of starting one, because you don't need cash and storage place to get started.

Downs: You stay responsible to get the product delivered, if it got lost in the mail you will have to get a new one delivered. Competition is high so your prices have to be low enough.

5 Handcrafted items/hobbies?

 Perhaps you have a great hobby, like making jewelry, art or clothing. Sell it online. You can market yourself on social networks, create a website to sell it from or sell it on sites like eBay. When you have a website, you can attract traffic by all the different methods mentioned in this book; social networks are also a good option for marketing. Not a bad choice, your hobby can be unique, and you can attract buyers who will love your art. People always like to have something unique and some always search for something unique. With attracting traffic to your site, you can start an excellent website about your hobby or handcrafted items.

Ups and downs selling your art ups: Brilliant idea to get your designs/art out to the public. It can become very popular, and you can become famous, who knows!

Downs: You'll have to create your art and run your website if your

Orders start to come in, make sure you will be able to handle it all.

6 ONLINE AUCTIONS

Online auction sites are not all working in the same way, some auctions are really tense. On some auction sites you pay-per-bid and on other auction sites you pay only for the item if you won the bid, pay per win. To pay per bid you pay credits. For some this might sound a little bit sceptic, there are sites selling all kinds of goods in a gamble manner. Why you might ask? Well the auction can get very addictive and very exciting to some. The advantage for the seller probably is that he/she can make more than was expected.

What are the risks?

Things to be aware of, on some auction sites you pay credits per bid (pay-per-bid) and a credit may vary in price, depending on which site you use. The bid will increase then by a small amount to the onlooker, which makes the item look very cheap indeed, but not for the bidder because you pay-per-bid, which means a bid can cost more money. Careful not to spend too much money on the item you are bidding on. Another downside on some auction sites, you lose your credits if you were not the winning bidder. So on the end you can get so carried away with the auction process and forget how much money you are spending. If you want to use auction sites that you pay only when you win the bid, you can walk away with a great bargain. When buying something on an auction you can't see the product and it stays a big gamble for the buyer. The item might not be in such a good condition as on the picture if you buy second hand items. In some cases the system is set up in a way that favours the seller, making it incredibly easy for a seller to defraud the buyer. Be sure what an item is worth, you don't want to end up paying too much. Set a limit on how much you want to spend on the item and be willing to lose the money if the auctioned item sells above your intended price (in cases of pay-per- bid auctions)

Ups and downs online auction

Ups: You can get a great deal, buy a bargain. Downs: Very addictive and you can get carried away, and pay too much.

7 PUBLISHING & PUBLISHERS

Ever thought of writing a book? With the internet and the increase of ebooks, it's much easier than you thought to write and publish an ebook. Reading will never die out, people just love to read a good story, get carried away in a good romance or fantasy. If you are not that type of writer, knowledge is also a great idea. People always want to read more about something they are interested in. There are lots of things to write about and all you have to do is to get thinking. A life experience or something about hobbies, cooking, decor, anything you have a passion about can turn into a book. There are sites that can helps you create and publish your eBook free. E-books are getting more popular, cheaper to buy and convenient. It stays an excellent opportunity to start writing.

Ups and downs publishing a book Ups: It can be something to be proud of, writing is being creative and that could be very rewarding. Downs: Writing your book might take a lot of time, writing your first book might even take a bit longer, because it is new to you. This might keep you busy a long time before earning anything.

8 AFFILIATE PROGRAMS

What is an affiliate program? Affiliate marketing in a nutshell means you direct your website visitors to products/services relating to what the topic of your website is. It's all about marketing, advertising goods or services and the business you referring your visitor to rewards you for each visitor you directed to them.

Few ways to help you with affiliate marketing is using:

8.1 Niches Niches are the keywords when searching the internet. A niche market is all about focusing on a particular market. An often used technique for affiliate marketers is Internet-based niche segments of larger markets, referred to as niches. A website can be developed and promoted quickly to serve a specific targeted customer, giving the affiliate a small source of income. This technique can then be repeated on several other niche websites. A bigger niche is harder to market, the expense of online advertisements increases according to the popularity of the keywords used (for example

AdWords). Find small, but still popular niches and remember to keep the focus on the market, product or service you want to attract. Your website should be all about the one specific market (that will be your niche), keep your site focused on one kind of market.

How do you make money using niches? Create a website focusing on a certain subject, for example cell phones, then refer your visitors to products and services that relates to that. You will get commission from the referrals.

8.2 Safelists

A safe list is basically a mailing list that is created especially for advertising websites, business opportunities, etc. All the members of a free or paid safelist agree to receive advertising emails from the other members. It benefits you by allowing you to advertise to the people on the safelist, via email or free ads. You can earn a commission too, but it stays hard work to earn that commission.

Ups and downs of affiliate programs

Ups: There is a significant variety of marketing; you can literally pick and choose which one you like best. Downs: It is hard work to get your traffic going and many scams to be looking out for.

9 BLOGGING

Blogging doesn't have to be like a diary; you can blog about anything. There are many sites where you can start your blog. Same applies for blogging as having a website; you need to advertise it and get traffic to make it successful enough to start earning money. Keep your topics interesting and something you have a great knowledge of. When your blog gets popular, you can start earning some cash. You can get sponsors relating to your subject, all depending on how popular your blog can get. If you are a blogger, getting a sponsor may be the best solution. You have control over who the sponsor is and someone who can best fit your blog's primary goals. A tried and true way to go about this is:

First and foremost, make sure your sponsor(s) can easily understand what he/she or they will be getting themselves into as well as what you are not looking for. Focus on the kind of services that you can offer to him/her or them. Do not hesitate to create a page for the rules of sponsoring your blog as well as to further promote them on social sites such as Facebook and Twitter.

Second, don't hesitate to try out a few to test what truly will work for you and your audience. Don't hesitate to set some deal breaker boundaries with your sponsor such as if they want to be users of your blog itself or not to allow your sponsor to be promoted on your blog itself.

Third, you will need to do your best to create the triple win situation for yourself, your sponsor(s) and your audience. First, think about the primary goals of your blog, whether it's to promote a product or service or whether you want to get paid in cash. Secondly, be clear with your sponsor(s) on what his/her or their goals are, whether it's to encourage free sign-ups for their product or re-direct your visitation traffic back to their website. Last but not least, also think about how your audience will benefit and whether one could be a potential sponsor.

Last but not least, do your research and make the triple win your main focus. Remember, you are helping to generate mutual revenue with your sponsor(s) so the last thing you ever want to do is make the mistake of being too promotional of your sponsor(s) and services.

Ups and downs of blogging

Ups: It can be fun having your blog, and if you are writing something you enjoy, you will love doing it every day.

Downs: Get it popular and get ads on your blog can be hard work.

10. Online videos

To put videos on YouTube may be a scary thought for some and an exciting idea for others. Your video doesn't have to be about you or something funny. If you can get a really good video out on you tube it can become popular, the more hits you get the more famous your video will get and who know how popular your videos will get. There are people who make a big income only from getting the right kind of videos on you tube. Many people were discovered on you tube, for example people with a talent. Most novice YouTube users mistakenly start on the bet that they will be able to make thousands of dollars by making their videos freely available throughout the Internet. Unfortunately, this is not so and most generate only about $1-$2 per a thousand views due to YouTube generating most of the

AdSense profits for itself.

Again, obtaining a sponsor may be your best solution. There are five types of sponsorships you can obtain for your video(s) depending on the specific goals you have: product assignment, brand combination, pre- and post-roll, banner promotion and endorsement.

If inserting your content within your video is what you're looking to do, it's a product assignment sponsor that you want. They typically offer the product and/or the cash for the product placement at the end of your advertisement, they can also help you save money if you're doing a fundraising placing ad with a large set of producers.

If doing a story around your product is more what you have in mind, it's a brand combination sponsor that you want. Basically the sponsoring company is included within the product. videomaker.com provides the example of the movie, The Internship, which not only centers on Google as part of the film's main plot but it was about the two main characters working for the company Google itself.

If you are looking to run 30-second advertisements in between your main video, it is the pre- and post-roll that you want. They can take on mainly any form that you desire for them to but beware that they may have their own rules and may try to place their advertisements during your main video.

If placing your ads at the bottom or somewhere within your video's website or somewhere visible on the screen during the video is what you are looking to do, it is banner promotion that you want. However, beware that some may place their advertisements without your consent and prevent you from having any say in the matter.

If you are looking for a company or organization who will simply fund your video, it is the endorsement (often referred to as underwriting) that you are looking for. The well-known television channel PBS for instance is an excellent example of someone who runs on various company contributions.

Some Other Basic Rules:

Content creators themselves are generally not allowed to sell the advertisements. If you use Facebook, you may be allowed to insert the advertisement content video but some sponsors may find this unattractive so it may be best to use someone who can show you the ropes around this.

Evaluate your content to ensure that it closely matches to what you are trying to help promote. For example, if your video is that of a model airplane, it could easily be used to promote specific brands of model airplanes or to advertise a collector's piece. This will determine who will be a good match for you as a sponsor.

Don't be afraid to seek out experts to help you evaluate your content. Generally, the more eyes that see it, the better chances you will have of making your content clean-cut enough to attract the sponsors and audience that you want.

Work with your sponsors and don't hesitate to seek out experienced videographers for advice on your advertising rates.

You'll then be ready to find your potential sponsors and start tracking your advertisements' effectiveness.

Ups and downs of online videos Ups: It could be fun to get creative and make the right video. Can get addictive when you see how many hits you have on your video, but it is fun. Downs: Not always easy to get a 'top hit' video, you might be lucky, not all videos going on you tube gets very popular, so advertise it, so your hits can grow. So it could take a few good videos before one get popular.

11. OFFERING A SERVICE

There is not one person who can do everything, which makes it easier for that person to offer services to people that can do whatever it is they would be offering. You could be proposing to create Photoshop images for a website, or even writing content. These people do not have the time or the patience to learn how to do these services so they will pay you for your time to help them complete their task. There are ways you can make money quickly within the first week. You could sign up for a freelancing website or you could go into detail by creating a website commercialization. You could also do social media marketing and marketing through email.

If you would rather not spend any money to make money, then signing up for freelancing sites would be the best way to go. All of their sites are free to register and you can choose from a plethora of jobs that appeal to you. During the registration process you would have to create a profile by putting up examples of some of your best work. This is how people will hire you for their service. If they like what they see after you complete your first task, they will have you complete more jobs so you can make even more money.

For these jobs, you would have to place a bid for the amount of money you think you deserve for that job. It has to be reasonable enough for people to accept your bid and hire you on to complete their task. It is important that you put down an email that you could check on a daily basis. That is how many of these people will let you know whether or not you have a job. Once you are hired to complete that task, they will let you know the amount of money they are paying you as well as when they need it buy so it is best to commit because you want to have a good reputation.

You may have a creative background and would like to create a website that explains the kinds of services you are selling. Each link you create will be like its own separate portfolio. For example, you may have a tab that says content where people can view samples of previous articles you have written. Or you might have a graphic design tab that may show business cards or flyers you have created either as a profession or just for fun. Do not forget to put how much you charge because many people may think you would offer a service for free.

One of the great things about creating a website is people know that you have website creating capabilities, and they may be able to use your help to set up their own. Another great thing is that you can use that to create your autobiography which lists the amount of experience you have working in each field you have mentioned on your website. By creating a website more and more people will be able to see it because you could advertise it on search engines. One of the reasons why many people create websites selling their services is there are some people that do not post jobs on freelance sites and you have to get your services out there.

There are many individuals who sell their services on social media websites by spending just a little bit of money to create advertisements listing the services they are selling. If you choose to go in that direction, then you could easily make the money back within your first week because there are a lot of people who could use help with several different tasks they are not able to complete. If you would rather not spend the money advertising, then you can also sell your services by creating posts or sending messages. None of your family or friends has to need anything, but they may know people who will charge you lots of money for your services. You would never know unless you experiment with it and give it a try.

Not that many people may think of selling their services through email, but it can be done. There are thousands of people who freelance and have their own website with their contact information.

You could send them an email and sell your services that way. They may have too much work that they can handle so they may hire you to help them out. You could also try emailing big corporations to sell your services, and that would look great on your resume if you were hired.

By signing up for freelancing websites, creating your own website, marketing through social media or email, you will be on your way to making a good living from home just by selling your services to people that need your help. To make even more money from home, it is important to expand your options meaning you could sell your services by taking advantage of all these different ways to promote your services. Be sure you mention where you would like your payment to be sent no matter which option you decide to do. Whether you choose to complete sign up process on freelancing sites or do some marketing in the most unique way possible; it will take some time. Fortunately it will be worth it when the payments start coming through.

12 Monetize contents

Turn your passion into profit through monetization. There are 4 main key players in a YouTube Monetization campaign. The first ones are the viewers. The viewers are the ones who will make it possible for you to gain income.

They are the ones who will click and watch the ads attached to your videos.

Second key players are the creators. The creators are the people who will create and upload videos and then monetize them to earn profit. They earn revenue by allowing YouTube to monetize their videos, which means that YouTube gets the right to add advertisements in their videos.

The third key players are the advertisers. The advertisers directly negotiate with YouTube, in which they pay an amount to play their ads in different videos uploaded on the site. The last player in the YouTube monetization is YouTube itself. YouTube platform negotiates with various advertisers to earn profit. They will then show these ads on the videos owned by the creators who will, in return, earn a share of the profit received by YouTube. YouTube gets to decide when and which video to show in a particular content.

Monetizing content is about allowing creators to earn money through the video clips they upload.

It gives YouTube the right to place advertisements on your videos. Those ads will be the source of your passive earning. You can activate your monetization properties by clicking on the "monetization tab" in your channel and then choosing the monetize-with-ads box. Monetize your content by first uploading it to your channel. After uploading, open your video manager and then

click the dollar ($) sign.

To validly monetize your videos, your content must be advertiser-friendly. This means that your video must not contain graphic or abusive materials that may give a bad reputation to the company advertising the product. YouTube has the right to decline monetizing a video clip that they find to be not advertiser-friendly.

Uniqueness of your content is also a must. By allowing your videos to earn money, YouTube is attesting that your videos are your own and that they contain no copyrighted materials. You must readily provide documentations as proof that you own the video and you own worldwide commercial right to all your video and audio contents.

Originality is an important aspect in monetizing since this will decide if your video will earn money or not. You can monetize videos you do not fully own as long as you have a written permission to do so. It is important to consider all the aspects of your video such as background music because these little things may cause revocation of monetization.

You can monetize videos of songs you originally wrote as long as you are not under a label company. If you have already signed a contract with a company, read the terms of your agreements first before monetizing your videos because some label may limit your commercial rights against your songs.

Uploading videos of public concerts, events and shows you personally filmed can be monetized as long as you have a written permission from the original owner. Even if you personally filmed such events, the original creator of those concerts or events hold certain rights to your content so you cannot commercially use it without asking for permission.

You are also not allowed to monetize videos you purchased. This means that even if you are authorized to upload songs you bought from iTunes, you cannot earn from it because YouTube will not allow you to monetize it. Before you are allowed to monetize, you have to ask for permission first.

Seek for a written authorization that states that the original owner of the content gives you the right to use it for commercial purposes.

If you created video tutorials for software use, you may or you may not monetize your video.

This will depend on the agreement you have with the licensed owner of the video. You can monetize the video if the original owner gave you the right to exploit the product commercially.

In some cases, a contract is drawn between you and the publisher which proves that you have paid a licensing fee. If you are asked by YouTube to provide information about the software you used in your content, you must readily give the name of the software and the link.

Some originally uploaded songs can also be monetized as long as the publisher claimed the song through content ID. If the song was not claimed, you are not allowed to monetize it unless you have a written permission to do so. So, to fully succeed in monetizing your video, you must maintain originality and uniqueness. If you are determined to monetize the videos of songs you covered, then better look for songs that were claimed or better yet directly contact the owner of the

song to ask for explicit permission to use their material. This may take a long time and hard work since it is hard to convince owners to just give you permission to use their songs for commercial purposes.

However, that is the thing about YouTube. It is hard to earn money that is why most YouTubers do not enter YouTube to gain; instead, they use it to share their passion. Some YouTubers are lucky and hardworking enough to earn a great amount of money. Learn a few more tips and you will surely succeed in this industry.

13 TEACHING AND TRAINING

There are quite some ways someone can make money online. Usually, people look towards making money with tried and true strategies such as network marketing, data entry, content writing, and personal assistant services. Anyone with any experience in these areas will quickly point out these are all useful means by which one can earn an income. For those with the right skills, there may be another way to make money online.

Offering teaching and training services can open numerous lucrative doors. The skill at the center of this potentially lucrative endeavor is teaching. Yes, those who have teaching skills can make quite a bit of money offering their services to those who are interested in accessing them. The truth is scores of the potential of customers are interested in taking online lessons from a good teacher.

To those who have never looked into how exactly teaching and training can be done via the internet might be quite surprised at the various skills that can be taught. Now, there are a few limitations that must be contended with. Not every skill can be taught online, but there are several that can be.

A cursory glance reveals courses in martial arts, cooking, foreign languages, home improvement, and more. Not all of these courses are accredited. As a source of learning, they can certainly prove extremely helpful. Those who enroll in an online education program can significantly enhance their skills far more than would be the case without any access to an online training course.

Imagine if you possessed great skill with mathematics. There is a huge demand for tutors and teachers do charge quite a bit of money per hour. If you were to develop a variety of learning and study guides for various basic or advanced math programs, a significant number of students might opt to sign up with what you are offering.

Creating a program for basic geometry could be quite easy. Ten half-hour lessons covering the standard material found n the first ten chapters of beginner geometry textbook can be recorded. Access to these videos could be stored on a private password protected section of a website. You never have to worry about how to set up a website as a design, development, and hosting service can handle all these tasks on your behalf.

Merely offering online lessons for a subscription is not the only component to earning money with this method. Tests could be made available, and you could grade them. One on one chats or even

Skype phone calls for tutoring and Q&A can be made available. A sliding scale of fees for different levels of teaching could be offered.

Of course, there are many various topics that can be offered beyond just geometry and math. Scores of academic, professional, and even hobbyist pursuits can be turned into a decent online training and teaching program.

No matter what type of program or topic you wish to teach, certain components will remain constant.

For one, you do have to have to be a proficient teacher. Those who enroll in the program you offer do have to learn something. Anyone who thinks they can haphazardly present some show and tell displays and think students will respond positively to them is mistaken. A lot of thought has to go into crafting a robust online training program. You do want your students to remain your students and continue to sign up for further lessons. You also want those students to speak highly of your service and write good reviews about it. And yes, reviews are bound to show up online be they pro or con. Apparently, you want the reviews to be good ones since they are the only reviews to sell your business.

Before you can have any students, however, you do have to engage in the necessary promotion of your endeavor. The way to go about doing this is not going to be terribly difficult to figure out.

Since you are planning on teaching online, you should take advantage of using the internet and the search engines to draw the necessary attention to your endeavor. Knowing the channels in which to promote is going to help the cause.

To a great extent, the promotional strategy to sell the online lessons must significantly stress the merits of the actual program. Since the material and your teaching style are what sell the program, you should offer insight to those who may prospectively be interested in it. A common strategy with the video files is to provide clips from the lessons on filing sharing sites such as

YouTube. Websites can also show text, images, and videos. Effective blogging can also be utilized to draw attention to the services you are offering.

Obviously, your material has to be impressive. If it is not, then the ability to bring in students is going to be tough. As a rule, you never want to advertise material to work against you.

There is one other major rule that has to be followed. Anyone offering a training program must have an enthusiastic customer base. Supplying information and knowledge to a niche can be lucrative, but if the niche is too small, then there are just going to be far too few customers in which to generate enough funds to cover the costs associated with launching the actual venture.

As long as the customer base is there and what you offer can be helpful to them, the chances of making money with online training programs are entirely possible.

Just be aware of the fact that a lot of work and effort is required to be successful.

14 CONTINUITY PROGRAMS AND MEMBERSHIP SITES

To those that are not familiar with the term "continuity program," do not fear. If you are not familiar with this term, then you are most definitely familiar with the term "do what you love and you will never work another day in your life." With this job ethos in mind, anyone considering starting a continuity program will find that they are engaging in an endeavor that not only will be fulfilling but will be rewarding financially.

An online continuity program is a program you set up online which provides a service, information or analysis which can be in the form of an online newsletter or webinar. You get paid through a monthly fee or subscription. You can design the schedule of your service, and your subscriber base grows about the quality and usefulness of the information that you are providing.

No one model works for all continuity designers and managers. To only say this is another way of making money online does not give continuity programs justice. If you prepare and organize your thoughts and engage in directed and proper research, then you will not simply find an online stream of income, but you may find your calling. The more successful continuity programs are the ones which are designed with passion, as well as finding a niche' which is marketable and can be expanded as oppose to just being trendy.

Begin With an Outline and a Mission Statement on What the Purpose and Goals of Your Continuity

Program Is

As in any business endeavor, one should write out what they have visualized the form of their business endeavor to take. A short mission statement of the stated goals and objectives of the desired continuity program will help one to focus on the essential elements to include in the program.

Select a Topic

This may be the hardest part for continuity program managers to do. Many may be tempted to go with the latest fad, trend or to try different programs by trial and error. What one really should do is to sit down and write down a list of at least three (3) and no more than ten (10) topics that one either already has a subject matter expertise, can quickly research and articulate a particular position or that one is deeply passionate about. The next step is to examine each topic and research each one extensively about the extent that the topics are already covered online through other programs and website programs. This will provide one with an indication whether the topic is already over marketed and whether your content and manner of delivery will be different enough to garner a loyal and expandable subscriber base.

When selecting your topic, you should also be honest about the relevance of your topic. You may have a deep passion about your topic, but it may not be elastic enough about content be marketable, let alone build a loyal expandable client base. Your research on existing online programs already covering your content should help you focus on which topics will be more viable.

One should try to select three (3) "finalist" topics to work on.

Manner of Delivery of Your Message is Important

The modern internet today provides us with various examples of content delivery. In designing a continuity program, one must take into consideration their individual communication style. For example, is one a more active writer or does one have a more established television presence?

This is important because the manner of your content delivery will help determine how effectively you are connecting with your subscribers. If one has never done a presentation in front of a camera in any form or manner, then one should not start right away in producing webinars until one determines they are comfortable with the medium.

Test Then Launch

Practice always makes perfect so before you launch a continuity program, begin with an analysis of your product. If you have never been in front of a camera, try a test webinar to see how you feel and what the video quality will look like online. Practice timing your presentation. Unless you have engaging content, a webinar of more than thirty minutes will be more than sufficient.

One should also create a test audience of family, friends, and co-workers to field feedback on your continuity program content. Remember to establish a broad sample of reviewers so you have varied constructive commentary.

Take your time to refine your product before you launch and do not be afraid to pull your product back, redraft it and launch again.

Set a Value for your Service and Build a Good Payment Option into Your Online Design before launching your product, set a value for a monthly subscription rate. Review similar content in the same industry and determine what subscribers are already accustomed to paying for content in your same industry and using the same method medium delivery. One should remember that the rate for a webinar does not have to be the same subscription price for an online newsletter.

15 AdSense

The advertisements are controlled and managed by Google, and web publishers only need to create a free AdSense account and copy and paste provided code to display the ads. Google

AdSense allows you to monetize your videos when viewers interact with the advertisement. It is a way to monetize your traffic and earn a share of the profit that Google gets from advertisers by displaying their ads on your contents. You will only earn once the viewer clicks on the advertisement or fully watches it.

Set up your Google AdSense by signing up and creating an account at the Google AdSense website. You need a PayPal or a bank account and mailing address before you can create an account. 18 years old and above are the only ones who are allowed to create so if you are younger than that, you will need to be parentally supervised.

There are various types of advertisements you can choose from. You can choose pre-roll ads that are shown on the beginning of your video. You earn from this ads per thousand of views so it is recommended to solidify your viewers first before monetizing your videos.

You can also opt for banners that are shown at the bottom of the video. You earn from banner ads on a per click basis. Some creators choose to use banners because these do not block the video completely. You should be careful in allowing pre-roll ads on your contents especially if your videos only last for a few minutes. No viewer would want to watch a one minute video with a 30-second advertisement attached to it.

Creators do not have direct control over the ads that are shown in their contents. This means that YouTube decides what to show in your videos. YouTube are also the ones who decide when and how many times the ads will be shown, which means that even if you monetize all your videos, it does not automatically translate that ads will be regularly shown in your contents. Though you have no control over this, you can block ads and exclude sensitive categories from appearing in your contents.

Keep in mind that Google AdSense does not allow you to have a steady stream of income.

Your earnings will depend on your traffic which is why earnings fluctuate from time to time. There will be times when you earn more than a hundred dollars but there will also be times when you earn nothing at all. Google AdSense is a long-term investment so you have to be patient and persistent.

The fastest way to earn money through Google AdSense is by building traffic. Encouraging more viewers to watch your videos regularly will help you earn more profit. Learn how to manage the ads in your contents. Experiment with advertisement sizes and style. Use smaller size of ads so that viewers will not be distracted. You can also change the contrast and color of your ads.

Some creators choose to use colors that are almost the same with their content so that the advertisement will naturally blend. On the other hand, other creators opt to use bright colors to make the ads stand out and grab more attention.

Experiment with these choices and find out which style suits your viewers and contents.

Be a YouTube Partner

The next step in earning money through YouTube is by partnering with YouTube. As a partner, you will take advantage of the different benefits offered by YouTube to its partners. You can freely and optionally be a part of the Partnership Program by applying to it. It is recommended to build a higher number of viewers and subscribers first before joining the partnership program.

To gain access to the YouTube Partnership Program, the program must be fully launched in your country. Your channel should be in good standing, which means that you haven't been physically challenged previously. You must also have a sufficient number of subscribers.

Partnering with YouTube will help you effectively and efficiently make money through advertisements that are displayed before and during your videos. It will also allow you to gain profit through paid subscriptions and merchandise and give you the chance to win prizes for the number of viewers you have. Partnering with YouTube will let you gain access to more content information tools that will be helpful in creating better channel and contents. Partners also have access to more and more community support groups that can help creators build a wider network. Community support groups will also help you with your problems and queries. The community is particularly helpful to beginners.

YouTube partnership provides convenience to creators since being a partner will allow you to build a worldwide audience. Your partnership will enable your contents to be on the top of the search results, which will give you more chance to increase your viewers. As a partner, your contents and your channel gain additional exposure through the extra promotion YouTube does.

As a partner, your uploaded contents will be rightfully yours. One perk of being a partner is that you will have a chance to own copyright and distribution rights on your original contents.

As a partner, you do not have to worry about the advertisements on your contents because Google will handle all ad placements, the collection of profit from advertisers and payments. Google will also match and decide which ads will be suitable for your contents. Your partnership will also allow you to keep track of your traffic and advertisement resources. Keeping track of your performance will help you learn to be more efficient in the future.

Another benefit is that you are not tied with YouTube because you have no exclusive agreement limiting you and your contents. This means that you will have more flexibility, which will allow you to gather more viewers outside

YouTube. You are not prohibited to show your videos on other video-sharing sites.

Find Outside Sponsorship

Sponsors are companies that will pay you to use their product or to promote their service. Finding sponsors is a hard task since they do not easily give the right to use their products. You have to be fully qualified to get a sponsorship. You can sign up with any sponsor you want and then wait for their response if they agree to have their products promoted by you.

Getting sponsorship depends on how large your traffic is. You must have a huge number of subscribers to get sponsorship approval. If you have already built a great number of subscribers, there is a high chance that sponsors will hire your service to promote their products. However, you can also find sponsors whom you think will match your contents. Look for a company that has premium products.

You can review the products of the company sponsoring you. Some channels post links and other information about their sponsor on the description box of their contents. Some creators even talk about their sponsors in the videos they create. Some sponsored videos might run in-video advertisements or use product placement.

Sponsorship is almost the same as affiliate marketing. In affiliate marketing, a business will let you market their products. By promoting their products, you can send traffic to their websites and in return, receive a commission on the sales made. Most of the time, creators add affiliate link to their video description.

You can market the product of your affiliate by recommending the products to your viewers.

You can also use the product in your video. Making a review on the product is also helpful since you will be discussing all the information about it.

As a creator, ensure that your contents match the specific affiliate program you joined. If you are into graphic designs tutorial, find an affiliate program related to your content. Do not promote beauty products in your design tutorials since will lead to confusion. If you are into TV show reviews, you can choose affiliate programs offered by TV show companies.

If you are into beauty tutorials, choose affiliate programs related to your content such as cosmetic companies, hair product enterprises, and others. In choosing a product, go for those that will give you one-time sale and those that will give you a steady stream of income.

After choosing a niche or an area of products you want to promote, find the proper keywords to use. Your keywords must not be complicated. It should be something people will use to find your content or affiliate product.

Do not forget to add the affiliate link in your video or in your description box. Affiliate marketing has been recommended by many

YouTubers since it provides higher income than AdSense. The great thing about affiliate marketing is that you earn a percentage of the sales as a commission. The rate usually ranges from 4% to 10%, which are actually pretty big especially if the products you sell cost hundreds of dollars.

Chapter 7: The Future

DEVELOP YOUR SKILLS

You need a business plan even for your small internet money making business. Whatever you choose to earn money, have a plan, know what you want to do, how you want to do it, what you are planning to make, how much you can invest in your new business. Know what your goal is with your new business even if you join an affiliate marketing program, know where you are going. You can only improve by playing on the web, start a web page, or register for some affiliate programs to see how it works for you. Get to know what kind of money making will work for you. If it doesn't work, don't see it as failing; see it is developing, because you gain more and more information. There is so much to learn on how to make money, but as you go on you'll develop your skills. Soon you'll learn what works best for you and how to improve on your 'business.' But you need to be in the game to learn best.

STOP WAISTING TIME

Start today if you want to make money, stop dreaming about it. No better time than the present, start looking around, getting ideas. Whatever you do, making silly mistakes in the beginning, etc., don't worry about that – that is also steps of learning. Important to know is how you want to make your money and start looking into that. Do your research and your business will grow sooner or later.

HOW TO START

After you planned your new online business and you know what you want to do to start making money, get on the web and do it. If you are interested in your online shop, get information on where to buy at retail prices, or where to find a trusted drop ship dealer. If you wish to own a website, search for free options to create a website and see what it looks like, get enough information to put on your website and remember to make it attractive. Now that you are set to get ads promote your site or online shop. Keep working on your site and enjoy your new business. If you are interested in getting a commission from affiliate programs, register today and follow their instructions on how to make money. First test it, to see if it is re- ally what you want to do to earn money. If you are interested in writing a book, write it first on your computer, if that is what you love to do, find a publisher online to publish your book. But start writing today, as it takes a lot of time to finish a book. If you are interested in blogging, or youtube, start a blog now find sites on the web to start a blog and write about something you have knowledge of or something you have an interest in. Let your imagination loose and write or get ideas for a video. When you are done, start working on advertising your 'business' and keep working, never give up. Put as much energy in this new online 'business as you possibly can. Keep doing research to keep improving your new online 'business.' Remember work hard, love what you are doing, keep learning to improve, and advertise.

HOW TO ATTRACT TRAFFIC

To draw traffic to your new website is always difficult. But with affiliate marketing, you can get your site where you want it. Remember to advertise your site is essential and hard work. You need to get traffic to your site to make it profitable. Here are a few ways to get traffic:

(a) There are companies (website promoters) that will offer you a service to pro- mote your site, it will cost you of course. Check enterprises that are doing web promotions.

(b) You can also check for free safe lists on the internet and start to advertise; it can be a lot of work. (safelists are part of affiliating marketing)

(c) Give the web user reason to come, if you put in the effort to provide out- standing up-to-date information on your site, people will come back more, increasing their chance of doing business with you. With other words make your website very attractive.

(d) Advertise, advertise, advertise is the answer to attracting traffic, just never give up! Try out all kinds of advertising you can get to get your website promoted.

(e) Advertise on social networks, tell everyone about your site, advertise everywhere.

(f) Make use of niches and Adwords/AdSense or find something similar. Even if you have to spend a little bit of money on getting your website promoted, it could be worth it at the end, because your site needs as much as possible traffic to make it work and make it successful. It is a lot of work, but as soon as you see the effects of your hard work, it will become worth it all.

Conclusion

Scores of folks dread mornings with the prospects of facing another prolonged day next to their boss. In the beginning, you most likely took pleasure in your job but at the moment you cannot wait for five o'clock to leave your boss. Every day people go through strenuous hours looking to make a living. Virtually, do employed guys acquire time to unwind and delight in their hard earned cash?

In the name of a career, many folks become strangers to their household members as a result of the unusual hours they go away and return again from work. To make things even worse, their personal monthly earnings are not equivalent to the time they devote working for their company. I think it is the time you got an alternative, and online working may be the best alternative.

Many workers are not rewarded well despite the hard work they invest in the office. Usually, the drawback doesn't set off right away, but it's a gradual process. The problem begins with criticism and lack of independence to do what you would like when you want to. This in the process leads to reduced work productivity and finally your career begins becoming a drag.

Online work permits you to organize your diary ultimately and even more, so it's incredibly satisfying, employment cannot offer the equivalent. Picture this; you put at the job to your own business. Besides working for someone else why don't you start out your own personal internet home-based business? It's about time you sack your employer and commence controlling your timetable.

Globalization and here am talking about the discovery of the web, has made it easy for any person to get started on a home business on the net. The internet is usually loaded with amazing online home business solutions that could make certain you earn a lifetime income. You can start online work with a small business in your free time, and once the bucks start coming in then, you might move on to full time. Regardless, you're better off being your boss as opposed to being employed by somebody else.

Most important, I can't emphasize it more, is to work hard, be creative and original. Don't think too big in the beginning, for instance, to see you as a millionaire within a month, stay realistic you can become very wealthy, but your business has to grow, and as you learn the skills, you will get better with time. Your new way of making money has to be a passion, something you love to do. Stay motivated and never give up. It may take years before you can be successful but don't forget you are working on your future, your own business, your success. Not all online businesses get successful at the same rate, so never be discouraged by that. If your 'business' fails miserably then try something new, and stay motivated, it wasn't a failure it was a learning experience. All your hard work will pay off eventually, just stay positive and never give up. Somewhere, somehow you will find your passion which will earn you money, just keep searching and trying which kind of online 'business' you can do to make your money. Hope your business is going to be a huge success, and my book helped you in some way to make your money making dreams come true. Best of luck with making your dreams come true.

Thank you again for taking your time to read this book

I hope this book was able to help you.

Thank you and good luck!

Technical Terms and Definition

IP address -That's your internet address. To connect a private network to the Internet requires using registered IP addresses to avoid duplicates. An IP address consists of 4 sets of numbers divided by three dots (for example 00.00.00.000)

Domain - A domain name refers to the web page. For example, www.example.com will be Example's website and www.info.ex- ample.com and www.store.example.com will be different web pages of Example.

Domain name - Domain names are used in URL to identify particular web pages. For example, in the URL http://www.example.com/index.html, the domain name is example.com

Domain hosting - Domain hosting refers to businesses that specialize in hosting domain names for individuals and companies. The hosting acts as a server for a particular website, the web host is what provides the content of web pages to the computer that want to access that page.

URL - Stand for Uniform Resource Locator, it is the global address on the world wide web (www) Example of a URL: http:/www.example.com/info.html The first part of the address is called a protocol identifier, and it indicates what protocol to use, the second part is referred to as a resource name, and it specifies the IP ad- dress or domain name where the resource is located.

Protocol - Protocol is the "language" computers use to communicate. There are different formats for example PPP/TCP/IP/SLIP/HTTP/FTP (the "P" on the end stands for protocol)

Cookie (not the type you can eat) - Information that the server saves, it keeps track of your movements on the site. Ideal for 'shop-cart' so you can always go back to where you were.

HTTP - Short for Hyper Text Transfer Protocol, the underlying protocol used by the World Wide Web (www). HTTP defines how messages are formatted and transmitted, and what actions web servers and browsers should take in response to various commands (for example http/www.example.com/info.html) The other main standard that controls how the World Wide Web works are HTML.

HTTPS - Short for Hyper Text Transfer Protocol Secure, basically the same as HTTP, but HTTPS have a secure delivery of site, used in banking, transferring money or where personal information, etc.

HTML - Short for Hyper Text Markup Language, the authoring language used to create documents on the World Wide Web.
HTML commands your web browser to dis- play text and graphics in an orderly fashion.

ICAP - Short for Internet Content Adaption Protocol is a protocol aimed at providing simple object-based content vectoring for HTTP services.

SCTP - Short for Stream Control Transmission Protocol. Focuses on the transport and session layers, rather the network layer.

FTP - Short for File Transfer Protocol. This is the protocol for exchanging files over the internet. Most commonly used to download a file from a server or to upload a file to a server.

E-commerce Or electronic commerce is for an online business making use of e-mail, instant messaging, shopping carts, web services, etc.

E-commerce is for an online business who deliver goods, services, and data and transmitting funds; it can be between 2 businesses or between an online business and customer.

Niche - Niche refers to a particular topic, subject or category. Web sites and blogs may pro- vide news and content on a niche (e.g. a blog about sports or finance), while online sellers often sell in niche categories. By focusing on a niche topic or category, you will see higher traffic numbers on your website or blog.

AdSense -The program is designed for website publishers who want to display targeted text or image ads on website pages and earn money when site visitors view or click the ads.

ISP - Short for Internet Service Provider, it refers to a company that provides Internet services, including personal and business access to the web.

PPC - Short for Pay Per Click, PPC is an internet marketing concept, the commission is made when an ad is clicked on, regardless if a sale is made or not. The site publisher would usually set a fixed pay per click rate.

CPC - Short for Post-Per-Click, an Internet marketing formula used to price online advertisements. Advertisers will pay the internet publishers according to the number of clicks a particular ad gets.

MLM - Short for Multi-Level-Marketing. A sales system where the salesperson receives a commission on his/her owns sales and a smaller commission on the sales from each person he/she convinces to become a salesperson.

Malware -
Malware is the broad term to describe any malicious software designed by hackers. Malware includes viruses, key loggers, zombie

programs, etc. Any software that can vandalize a computer, steal someone's private information, take remote control of a computer, manipulate you into purchasing something, are called malware.

FFA - Short for Free For All. FFA web pages contain a collection of indiscriminate, often unrelated, links to other websites.

Opt-in - To accept a situation or condition ahead of time. For example, to opt-in to an e-mail marketing company means that you want to receive information regarding that company or from third parties. You can cancel the service anytime. Spamming is sent out using opt-in as an excuse that you did opt-in at some stage.

Opt-out - Opt-out is to stop some service or condition.

Outbound Link - A link from one website to a different website.

Text Link -A word or few words in hypertext, it connects one area of a web page with another area or with another web page.

Traffic - That is the amount of information being transferred. When you visit a website and download any of its pages, then it is causing "traffic" - information is being transferred between the website and your computer.

XML - Short for Extensible Markup Language, a cousin of HTML. XML focused on cataloging and organized storing of the text content of a web page.

ZIP - Windows file in a compression format. Usually, big files that are compressed to be downloaded faster. A file that is compressed will end on".zip."

www.ingramcontent.com/pod-product-compliance
Lightning Source LLC
Chambersburg PA
CBHW060349190526
45169CB00002B/544